Mat

The novice version

L. C. Norman

CAMBRIDGE
UNIVERSITY PRESS

Published by the Press Syndicate of the University of Cambridge
The Pitt Building, Trumpington Street, Cambridge CB2 1RP
40 West 20th Street, New York, NY 10011–4211, USA
10 Stamford Road, Oakleigh, Melbourne 3166, Australia

© Cambridge University Press 1994

First published 1994

Printed in Great Britain at the University Press, Cambridge

A catalogue record for this book is available from the British
Library

Library of Congress cataloguing in publication data
Norman, L. C.
Mathland: the novice version / L. C. Norman
    p.   cm.
1. Mathematical recreations – Juvenile literature. 2. Problem
solving – Juvenile literature. [1. Mathematical recreations.
2. Problem solving.] I. Title.
QA95.N583 1994
793.7'4 – dc20 94-15711 CIP

ISBN 0 521 46801 9 paperback

Cover illustration and cartoons by Simon Larkin

INSTRUCTIONS

There are detailed instructions on the next two pages.

READ THEM CAREFULLY BEFORE YOU ENTER MATHLAND.

Some of the pages have boxes. These are for you to explore when you have finished travelling through Mathland.

You enter the maze at the Gate of Hope.

There is a clap of thunder, and the Magic Mathematician stands before you.

'You will be given a set of problems to solve,' he explains. 'If you are successful, you will gain points. If you are stuck, you may pay points to receive help. Your answers will guide you to the next stage of the maze.'

Use the **map sheet** to make a map of your route through the maze. Alternatively, you could use a sheet of A4 paper. Start on the left of the page, about 12 cm up from the bottom. Use a scale of 1 cm to 1 mile.

Your map should include the names of the places you visit. You will receive help with the map along the way. The roads between places will always be straight – but your path may double back on itself.

You should also record the pages you visit, in the order you visit them. Then, if you lose your way, you will not have to start again at the very beginning.

Finally, there is space on the map sheet for you to record the points you win and lose.

You notice the rays of the Sun being reflected from the top of a tall tower. You decide to investigate . . .

Start on page **11**.

Good luck!

YOU SHOULD NOT BE READING THIS PAGE.

You were told to start on page **11**.

Turn back to the Instructions and read them again, more carefully this time.

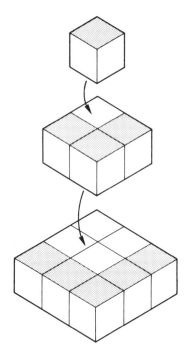

Take the tower apart.

How many cubes do you have?

Make it with multilink cubes, and count.

▶▶ 3

Turn left.

Continue on your journey for 4 miles.

You reach the Ridge of Ramanujan, where you are greeted by a friendly rabbit.

'Three roads meet at this Ridge,' explains the rabbit. 'So, to decide which road to take, I could toss 2 coins. I would either get:

> 2 heads
> or 2 tails
> or 1 head, 1 tail.

'That would be a fair way of choosing the road, wouldn't it?'

Yes ▶▶ 17
No ▶▶ 10

4

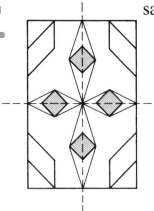

'There are 2 mirror lines,' says the ant.

'Now, can you tell me how many mirror lines there are on my admirable carpet?'

Take your answer, multiply it by 5 and subtract 1 and turn to that page ▶▶

If stuck ▶▶ 25

You turn through 180°, and retrace your steps to the Ridge of Ramanujan.

CHECK YOUR MAP

'Another puzzle?' requests the rabbit.
'Take the digits:

9 8 7 6 5 4

'Make two 3-digit numbers, so that they make the *smallest* (positive) answer when one is subtracted from the other.'

Take the digits of your answer, multiply them together and turn to that page ▶▶

If stuck PAY 10 POINTS ▶▶ 27

6

Any number ought to work.
Go back to **31** and try again.

If you are still stuck – ask for help.

The factors of 6, apart from itself are 1, 2 and 3.
If you add all of these factors together, you get back
to the original number:

$$6 = 1 + 2 + 3.$$

Numbers like this are called perfect numbers.
Can you find the next perfect number? It is less
than 30.
How about the next one? It is less than 500!

'Imagine taking the tower apart,' explains the giraffe.

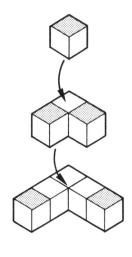

Top layer – 1 cube

Middle layer – 3 cubes

Bottom layer – 5 cubes

That makes 9 cubes in all.

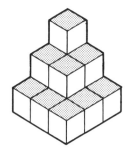

'Now try again,' suggests the giraffe. 'How many cubes?'

Take your answer and turn to that page ▶▶

If stuck ▶▶ 2

8

LOSE 10 POINTS

'You probably need to think some more about this problem,' ruminates the rabbit. Was your fraction in its simplest terms?

If not, go back to **17** and try again.

If stuck  13

Can you put 8 queens on this chessboard so that no piece is attacking any other piece? (That is, you must not have two pieces on the same row, column or diagonal.)

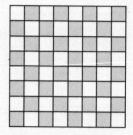

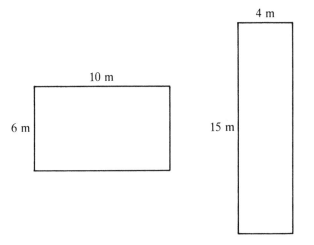

Think of different sizes of fields which have an area of 60 square metres – like the ones here.

Now find one which has a perimeter of 34 metres.

When you have your correct field, take the small side away from the large side, multiply your answer by 5 and turn to that page ▶▶

If still stuck ▶▶ 33

You explain to the rabbit that there are four possible outcomes:

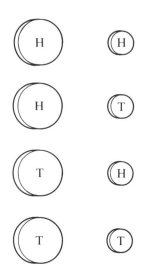

So the rabbit is most likely to get 1 head and 1 tail.

SCORE  30 POINTS

▶▶ 13

You head south for 4 miles till you reach the Tower of Galileo. You are greeted by a tall giraffe.

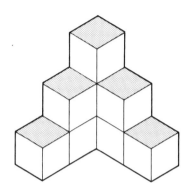

'How many cubes are there in my tall tower?' gurgles the giraffe.

Take your answer, double it and turn to that page ▶▶

If stuck PAY 10 POINTS ▶▶ 7

12

'Well done!' cries the rabbit. 'The probability of getting an even number is $\frac{1}{2}$.'

SCORE **20** POINTS

▶▶ 13

Srinivasa Ramanujan (1887–1920) was a brilliant, basically self-taught, mathematician. He was the first Indian to be elected to the Royal Society.

You make your way north. After 3 miles you reach the Arch of Archimedes.

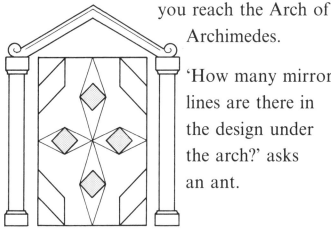

'How many mirror lines are there in the design under the arch?' asks an ant.

Take your answer, multiply it by 8, and turn to that page ▶▶

If stuck PAY 10 POINTS ▶▶ 4

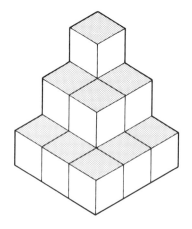

'Well done!' giggles the giraffe. 'There are 14 cubes.'

'Right,' roars the rabbit.

        654
      − 123
        531 is the largest answer.

SCORE 30 POINTS

▶▶ 31

Galileo Galilei (1564–1642) supported the idea that planets revolved around the Sun (and not that everything revolved around the Earth). This caused him to be accused of heresy by the Church.

He is supposed to have dropped objects from the top of the Leaning Tower of Pisa to show that they reached the ground at the same time: that is, they had the same acceleration.

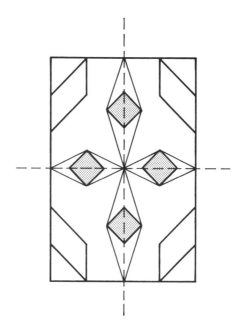

'Admirable,' admits the ant. 'There are
2 mirror lines.'

SCORE 30 POINTS

▶▶ 5

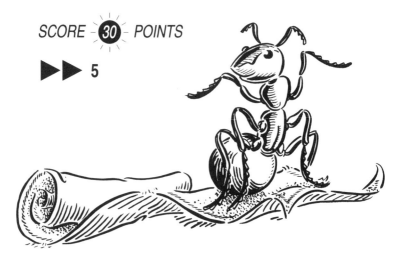

The rabbit is wrong – there are four possible outcomes:

So the rabbit is most likely to get 1 head and 1 tail.

'Try this problem instead,' says the rabbit. 'If I roll a 6-sided fair die, what is the probability that I will roll an *even* number?'

Write your answer as a fraction $\frac{?}{?}$. Then write the top and the bottom next to each other, and turn to that page ▶▶

For example: $\frac{3}{4}$ ▶▶ 34

If stuck ▶▶ 8

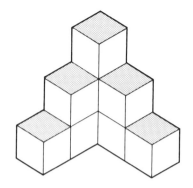

'Correct, 9 cubes,' gloats the giraffe.

SCORE **30** *POINTS*

▶▶ 3

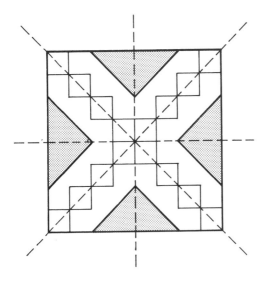

'Four mirror lines,' agrees the ant.

SCORE **20** *POINTS*

▶▶ 5

'Find the size of my field,' trumpets the elephant. 'The area of the field is 60 square metres. The perimeter (distance all round) of the field is 34 metres.'

When you have your answer, take the small side away from the large side, multiply your answer by 5 and turn to that page ►►

If stuck PAY 10 POINTS ►► 9

'Ridiculous to give up!' roars the rabbit.

$$
\begin{array}{r}
654 \\
-123 \\
\hline
531
\end{array}
$$

'is the largest answer you can make.'

▶▶ 31

Fibonacci numbers start:

1, 1, 2, 3, 5, 8, 13, 21, . . .

What is the rule for finding the next number?

Fibonacci numbers occur frequently in Nature (count the petals on flowers or the spirals on a pine cone).

'Hello again,' trumpets the elephant. 'I have a number puzzle for you this time.'

Choose any three digits.

Arrange them to make the largest possible number.

Now use them to make the smallest possible number. Subtract your two numbers (largest − smallest).

Look at your answer and repeat the process.

Continue until you get the same answer twice in a row.

Add the digits of your answer together, add thirty, and turn to that page ▶▶

If stuck PAY 10 POINTS ▶▶ 46

'If you don't like my hexagons, you had better be on your way,' buzzes the bee. 'Fly east for 8 miles and return to the Earthworks of Euclid.'

CHECK YOUR MAP

 ▶▶ 22

If there are 23 or more people in a room, the probability that at least two of them have the same birthday is greater than $\frac{1}{2}$ (more than an even chance).

'You thought right,' roars the dragon.

SCORE **30** *POINTS*

Turn south and continue for 6 miles. You are greeted by an elephant at the Earthworks of Euclid.

 20

Euclid lived about 300 B.C. in Alexandria when Ptolemy the First was Pharaoh. He is known for his book on geometry, called the *Elements* – which must be the best-selling maths book of all time. It tells you all you could want to know about triangles, circles and parallel lines.

'My admirable square carpet has 4 mirror lines,' admits the ant. 'Don't you like symmetry?' asks the ant. 'Maybe you will find the other problems easier.'

▶▶ 5

Archimedes (about 287–212 B.C.) lived in Syracuse in Sicily. He showed that the purity of a gold crown could be found by weighing the crown, and by finding how much the level went up when it was placed in water (a way of finding its volume). Archimedes is supposed to have thought of this idea while taking a bath. Legend has it that he then ran naked into the street, crying 'Eureka' (I've found it)!

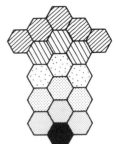

You are buzzed by a busy bee. 'Look at my honeycomb – it grows out in layers.
There are 6 hexagons round the edge of the smallest comb. How many are there round the edge of the largest comb?'

Take your answer and turn to that page ▶▶

If stuck PAY 10 POINTS ▶▶ 37

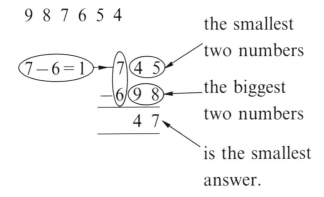

9 8 7 6 5 4

the smallest
two numbers

7 − 6 = 1 → 7 (4 5)

the biggest
−6 (9 8)
two numbers

4 7

is the smallest
answer.

'Try again,' rumbles the rabbit.
Take the digits:

1 2 3 4 5 6

Make two 3-digit numbers, so that they
make the *largest* (positive) answer when
one is subtracted from the other.

Take the digits of your answer, multiply them together
and turn to that page ►►

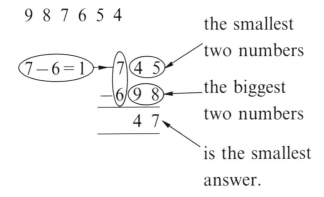

If stuck ►► **21**

27

'Right,' roars the rabbit.

$$745$$
$$-698$$
$$47$$ is the smallest you can get.

SCORE 30 POINTS

▶▶ 31

1, 3, 6, 10, 15, 21, 28, . . .

Why are these numbers called triangle numbers?

What sort of numbers do you get if you add neighbouring triangle numbers together?

1 + 3, 3 + 6, etc.

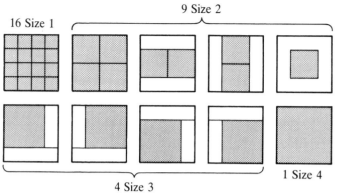

16 Size 1

9 Size 2

4 Size 3

1 Size 4

'Fabulous,' agrees the frog, '30 squares.'

SCORE – *30* – POINTS

'Now turn through 180° and hop along for 3 miles.'

▶▶ 67

'Brilliant,' buzzes the bee, '30 hexagons.'

SCORE **30** *POINTS*

'Now fly east for 8 miles, and return to the Earthworks of Euclid.'

CHECK YOUR MAP

▶▶ 22

You turn left, and continue for 4 miles. You are alarmed to meet a dragon which is guarding the Door of Descartes.

'Think of a number!' commands the dragon. 'Multiply it by 100, add 1993, take away your first number.'

Add the digits of your answer together and repeat until you have a single digit.

Multiply your answer by 6 and turn to that page

If stuck PAY 10 POINTS ▶▶ **6**

32

'Bravo!' triumphs the elephant.

'You end up with the digits 4, 5 and 9.'

SCORE *POINTS*

You move north for 6 miles.
You should reach the Door of Descartes.

CHECK YOUR MAP

 ▶▶ 41

'You can't have tried enough fields,'
trumpets the elephant in exasperation.
You turn right and keep straight for
8 miles.

You hear a buzzing noise ahead as you
approach the Hive of Hippocrates.

 26

Hippocrates of Chios lived in about 460 B.C. His work
on geometry was completed nearly one hundred years
before that of Euclid.

34

'You've done it!' lauds the lobster. 'They need 7 journeys.'

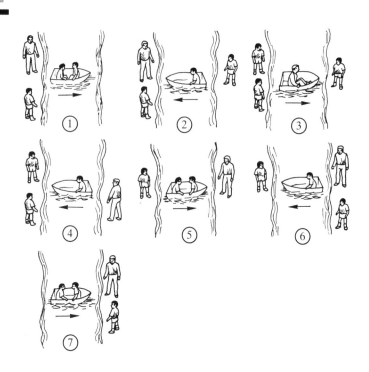

SCORE **20** *POINTS*

▶▶ 36

'Exactly right,' exclaims the elephant.

You turn right and keep straight for
8 miles.

You hear a buzzing noise ahead as you
approach the Hive of Hippocrates.

▶▶ **26**

36

You turn left and continue for 4 miles. At the Cliff of Copernicus you are greeted by a clever cat. 'Can you solve my code?' purrs the cat. 'It tells you which page to go to next.'

TOFSUPOERARVNGTETEYN

'I'll give you a clue,' continues the cat, 'think about factors.' ▶▶

If stuck PAY 10 POINTS ▶▶ 61

How many hexagons round the edge here?

And round the edge here?

Now draw the next layer and find the pattern.

 Work out how many there will be round the edge here.

Take your answer, and turn to that page

If stuck ▶▶ 23

'Dead right,' dribbles the dragon.

$$\frac{2}{3} = 0.666...\ \leftarrow\text{the biggest}$$

$$\frac{3}{5} = 0.6$$

$$\frac{5}{8} = 0.625$$

SCORE 20 POINTS

▶▶ 50

'Have you tried *all* the factor pairs?' chides the cat crossly. 'I know that one pair would work.'

You go north for 3 miles.

You hear a splashing noise and reach the Fountain of Fibonacci.

▶▶ 65

Leonardo of Pisa (Fibonacci) (about 1170–1240) made the Arabic numerals (1, 2, 3,...) generally known in Europe.

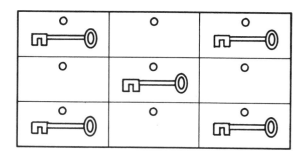

'Perfectly right,' puffs the perch. 'You might choose the 4 empty boxes first – so you need 5 boxes to be sure.'

▶▶ 71

'Hello again,' drools the dragon. 'I have three cakes here. They have been cut into slices. Which cake has the biggest fraction left?'

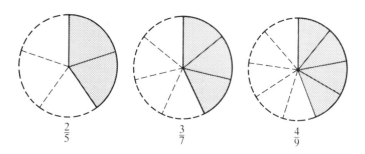

$\frac{2}{5}$ $\frac{3}{7}$ $\frac{4}{9}$

Find the largest fraction and write it like a number (for example, $\frac{3}{4} \rightarrow$ **34**).

Turn to that page ►►

If stuck PAY 10 POINTS ►► 55

'Lovely,' laughs the lobster.

F | C
LG →
(1)

F | C
← L
(2)

G F
LC →
(3)

G F
← LG
(4)

C

G
LF →
(5)

C G
← L
(6)

F | C
LG →
(7)

F | C

L = Lobster
C = Cabbage
F = Fox
G = Goose

'It takes 7 journeys.'

SCORE **30** POINTS

▶▶ 36

43

'Since you can't work it out, the man and boys will just have to walk all around the lake,' laments the lobster.

 36

Joseph-Louis Lagrange (1736–1813) was one of the greatest mathematicians of the eighteenth century. He published a book summarising all the work done on mechanics (how things move) in the 100 years since Newton. He studied wobbles in the Moon's orbit and developed his own system for describing the movement of planets etc.

LOSE 10 POINTS

Suppose you had £120.

$\frac{1}{3}$ of 120 is £____ , so $\frac{2}{3}$ is £____ .

$\frac{1}{5}$ of 120 is £____ , so $\frac{3}{5}$ is £____ .

$\frac{1}{8}$ of 120 is £____ , so $\frac{5}{8}$ is £____ .

Now which is biggest?

 50

René Descartes (1596–1650) is the father of modern-day philosophy. He tried to explain all natural events in one single system of mechanical rules. He is known for the phrase 'I think, therefore I am.'

'Think about the different possible sizes of triangle,' suggests the frog.

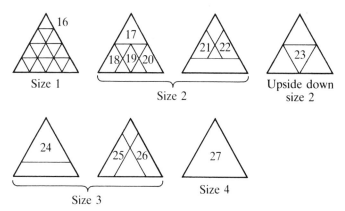

Size 1

Size 2

Upside down size 2

Size 3

Size 4

'You have 27 triangles altogether.

'Maybe you think better in squares,' continues the frog. 'How many squares – little, medium and big – are there altogether here?'

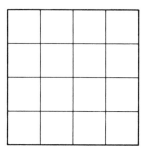

Take your answer, subtract 1 and turn to that page ▶▶

If stuck ▶▶ 68

46

Suppose you chose the digits

　　　1　　　6　　　9

The largest number you can make is 961 and the smallest is 169.

Subtract them:　　961
　　　　　　　　　－169
　　　　　　　　　 792

Now do the same with the digits

　　7　　　9　　　2

Carry on until you get the same answer twice in a row.

Add the digits of your answer together, double it, subtract 4 and turn to that page ▶▶

If stuck ▶▶ 53

'Clever clogs,' chuckles the cat. 'You cracked the code.'

SCORE 30 POINTS

Go north for 3 miles.

You hear a splashing noise and reach the Fountain of Fibonacci.

▶▶ 65

Nicolaus Copernicus (1473–1543) was a famous astronomer who first came up with the idea that the Earth moved around the Sun (not the other way round).

'Bravo,' triumphs the elephant.

$$4 + 5 + 9 + 30 = 48$$

SCORE POINTS

You move north for 6 miles. You should reach the Door of Descartes.

CHECK YOUR MAP

▶▶ 41

48 is an abundant number – it is less than the sum of its factors (not including itself).

$$1+2+3+4+6+8+12+16+24=76$$

Find some other abundant numbers under 100 (there are 21 of them).

'Dead right,' dribbles the dragon.

$\frac{2}{5}$ is 0·4.

$\frac{3}{7}$ is 0·42857...

$\frac{4}{9}$ is 0·44444... and so is the biggest.

SCORE **30** *POINTS*

▶▶ **50**

You continue north for 6 miles until you reach the shores of Lake Lagrange.

A large lobster stands at the edge of the lake. At its feet sit a fox, a goose and a cabbage.

'I must ferry these across the lake,' laments the lobster. 'My boat is only big enough for myself and one passenger. But if I leave them alone, the fox will eat the goose and the goose will eat the cabbage.

'What is the smallest number of journeys I need to make back and forth across the lake?' (There and back counts as two journeys.)

Take your answer, multiply it by 6 and turn to that page ►►

If stuck PAY 10 POINTS ►► 70

'Wasn't 64 on your lists?' nudges the newt.

'It was on mine.

'You must have nearly reached the end of your journey. Head south for 3 miles.'

 72

Find successive powers of 2:

$$2, 2^2 (= 2 \times 2), 2^3 (= 2 \times 2 \times 2), 2^4, 2^5 \ldots$$

Look at the pattern in the last digit.

Do the same for powers of 3, 4, . . ., 9.

Make a list of your findings.

52

'Three cheers for you!' exclaims the cat.

'The kittens must have had 12 mice. So I had 36 mice and gave 36 to the dog – that makes 72 mice to begin with. Yum, yum!'

SCORE 30 POINTS

▶▶ 69

52 is the number of weeks in the year.

52 is the number of playing cards in a pack (not counting jokers) divided into 4 suits of 13 cards.

53

'You should have kept trying,' exclaims the elephant.

'Now you must carry on with your journey.'

You move north for 6 miles. You should reach the Door of Descartes.

CHECK YOUR MAP

 41

53 is a prime number – its only factors are 1 and itself. The prime numbers can be found using the sieve of Eratosthenes.

Write down all the numbers (say) from 1 to 100. Put a cross through every 2nd number to get rid of multiples of 2 (but do not cross out 2 itself).

Put a cross through every 3rd number to get rid of multiples of 3 (but do not cross out 3 itself).

Carry on until you can't do any more. Any number left will be prime.

'Fantastic!' cries the frog. 'There are 27 triangles.'

SCORE **30** POINTS

'Now turn through 180° and hop along for 3 miles.'

▶▶ **67**

'Use fraction strips or turn the fractions into decimals,' explains the dragon.

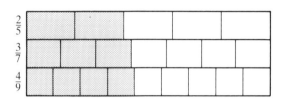

$$\frac{2}{5} = 2 \div 5 = 0{\cdot}4$$

$$\frac{3}{7} = 3 \div 7 = 0{\cdot}42857 \ldots$$

$$\frac{4}{9} = 4 \div 9 = 0{\cdot}4444 \ldots \text{ the biggest.}$$

'Try again – which of these is biggest?'

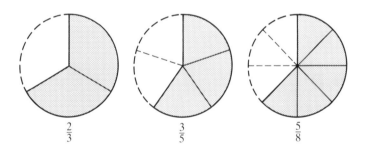

$$\frac{2}{3} \qquad \frac{3}{5} \qquad \frac{5}{8}$$

Take your answer, write it like a number (for example, $\frac{2}{7} \rightarrow$ **27**) add 15 and turn to that page ►►

If stuck ►► **44**

56

'Perfectly correct,' puffs the perch. 'Your first 5 strings had a dead fish on the end. But the 6th had a key.'

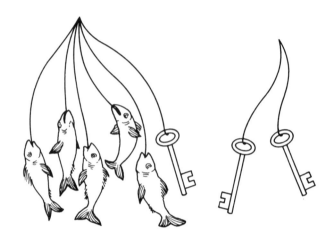

SCORE ·**30**· POINTS

 71

'In mathematics,' maintains the Magic Mathematician, 'it often pays to observe things from more than one direction.'

Does your map tell you which way to turn now?

Yes ▶▶ 76
No ▶▶ 75

Can you turn this pile of coins upside down, by moving just 3 coins?

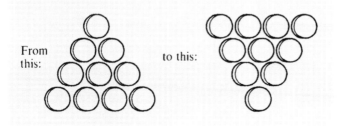

From this: to this:

2	9	4
7	5	3
6	1	8

'Marvellous,' mumbles the millipede. 'Your square could be this one turned round or flipped over.'

SCORE **30** *POINTS*

For the last stage of your journey you head east for 8 miles.

▶▶ **79**

'Imagine the worst,' explains the perch. 'There are only 3 keys – so your first 5 strings might each have a dead fish on the end.'

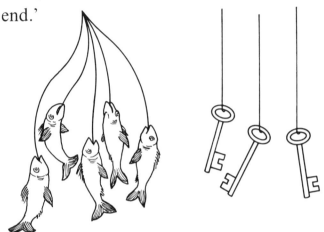

'So you need 6 strings to be sure.

'There are 5 more keys in these 9 boxes,' continues the perch. 'What is the smallest number of boxes you must open to be sure of finding a key?'

Take your answer, multiply it by 8, and turn to that page ▶▶

If stuck ▶▶ 73

60

'Well done!' purrs the cat. 'The rabbit had 9 balls. So I must have had 45 balls after I lost some. That was three-quarters of what I started with – so I had 60.'

SCORE -⚡30⚡- POINTS

▶▶ 69

Where do we use 60 (and multiples of 60) in real life?

Try this code:

CEMAAENDSYTSOHAUIGRSE

1 Count the number of letters – 21.
2 Think of all the factors of this number (not itself) – 3 × 7 or 7 × 3.
3 Then split the message in these different ways:

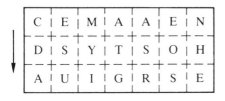

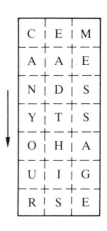

Read downwards – this is still gibberish!

This makes sense!

Now try again!

TOFSUPOERARVNGTETEYN

If you have cracked the code ▶▶

If stuck ▶▶ 39

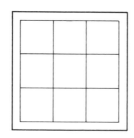

62

1 2 3 4 5 6 7 8 9

Try putting the middle number in the middle square.

$$1 + 2 + 3 + 4 + 5 + 6 + 7 + 8 + 9 = ?$$

So all the numbers in the square add up to **?**

How much will each row or each column add up to?

Now try and fill in the rest of the numbers.

When you have your square, multiply the four corner numbers together, divide by 8, then add 10. Turn to that page ▶▶

If stuck ▶▶ 74

You turn

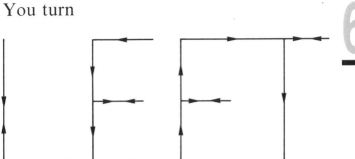

and enter through the Gate of Wisdom.

Your task is completed!

Work out your final score ▶▶ 80

64

'Nicely done,' nods the newt.

64 is 8×8 and $4 \times 4 \times 4$.

SCORE *POINTS*

Now head south for 3 miles ►► 72

Sir Isaac Newton (1643–1727) was one of the best known mathematicians and scientists.

His theory of mechanics (how things move) was unchallenged for three hundred years.

> Nature, and Nature's laws lay hid in night:
> God said, *Let Newton be!* and all was light.
>
> Alexander Pope

A frisky frog is sitting by a fountain of triangles.

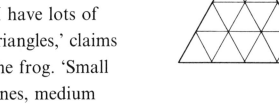

'I have lots of triangles,' claims the frog. 'Small ones, medium ones and large ones.

'How many triangles are there altogether?'

Take your answer, double it and turn to that page ▶▶

If stuck PAY 10 POINTS ▶▶ 45

LOSE 10 POINTS

'That rabbit is cleverer than I thought,'
muses the cat.

▶▶ **69**

The factors of 66 are:

1, 2, 3, 6, 11, 22, 33, 66.

Add them all up, and you get a square number:

$$1+2+3+6+11+22+33+66=144=12\times12$$

Find some more numbers with this property (three are
less than 66).

You return to the Cliff of Copernicus.

CHECK YOUR MAP

'We meet again,' mews the cat. 'I have a nice mice problem for you.

'I have some mice.

I give half to my friend the dog.

I give one third of those left to my kittens, and I eat the rest.

Three-quarters of the kittens' mice run away.

They are left with 3 mice.

How many mice did I start with?'

Take your answer, subtract 20 and turn to that page ►►

If stuck PAY 10 POINTS ►► 77

LOSE 10 POINTS

'Have I still fooled you?' frowns the frog. 'I thought that squares would be easier than triangles.'

'Now turn through 180° and hop along for 3 miles.'

▶▶ 67

```
            1
         1     1
      1     2     1
   1     3     3     1
1     4     6     4     1
```

This triangle of numbers is known as Pascal's triangle. Fill in the next two layers. Find out more about Pascal's triangle.

Turn right through 90°. Move forward for 4 miles. A perch is sitting in the Pool of Poisson.

'There are 8 strings here,' pouts the perch.

'Three of them have a key attached to the end. What is the smallest number of strings you must pull from the pool to be sure of picking a key? (You are allowed just one turn.)'

Take your answer, multiply it by 9, then add 2 and turn to that page ▶▶

If stuck PAY 10 POINTS ▶▶ 59

'The trick,' laughs the lobster, 'is to leave the two things which don't eat each other together. You take the goose across, and later you bring it back again.'

F	LG →	F	L ←
C	①	C	②

G F	LC →	G F	LG ←
	③		C ④

G	LF →	C G	L ←
	⑤		F ⑥ C

LG →	F
⑦	C

L = Lobster
C = Cabbage
F = Fox
G = Goose

'See if you can help these people now' asks the lobster. 'There are 3 boys and 1 man. Their boat can only take 1 man or 2 boys. How many journeys, back and forth, do they need to cross the lake?'

Take your answer, multiply it by 5, subtract 1 and turn to that page ▶▶

If stuck ▶▶ 43

Turn clockwise through 90°. Move forward 10 miles. You find a newt sitting under the Apple tree of Newton.

'I have a number puzzle,' nods the newt. 'Find the smallest number (not 1) which is a perfect square *and* a perfect cube. (For example, $25 = 5 \times 5$ is a perfect square; $8 = 2 \times 2 \times 2$ is a perfect cube.)'

Take your answer and turn to that page ▶▶

If stuck PAY 10 POINTS ▶▶ 78

LOSE 10 POINTS

You reach the Mount of Maxwell.
A millipede crawls at the foot of the
mountain. 'Make me a magic square,'
mouths the millipede.

Take the numbers 1 to 9.

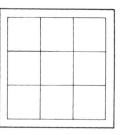

Fit them into this square
so that each row, each
column and both
diagonals all add up to the same total.

You may only use each number once.

When you have your square, take the four
corner numbers, multiply them together, divide by 8, then
add 10 and turn to that page ▶▶

If stuck PAY 10 POINTS ▶▶ 62

'It's perfectly simple,' pouts the perch. 'I think you have just decided to give your brain a rest.'

 71

Siméon-Denis Poisson (1781–1840) used mathematics in the study of electricity, magnetism, mechanics, and other areas of physics. He developed the idea that electricity is made up of two fluids, in which like particles repel each other and unlike attract.

LOSE 10 POINTS

'You must have given up too soon,' mumbles the millipede.

For the last stage of your journey, you head east for 8 miles.

 79

James Clerk Maxwell (1831–1879) developed a set of equations which are the basis for the study of electricity, magnetism, radio waves, light, etc.

Your map is not sufficiently clear for you to enter the Gate of Wisdom.

You must return to the Gate of Hope, and rechart your progress through the maze. You do not need to solve the problems again – use your list of pages visited to help you redraw the map.

Can you find someone to help you discover what went wrong?

 11

Score each letter of your word thus:

A B C D... Z
1 2 3 4 ... 26

Find the total score of your word, add 20 and turn to that page ▶▶

If stuck ▶▶ 57

Start at the end!

3 mice is one quarter of the kittens' share. So the kittens had 12 mice.

So I had 36 mice, after I had given some to the dog – which makes 72 mice to begin with.

'Now solve this one' mews the cat.

I have some ping pong balls.

I lose one quarter of them.

I give one fifth of what is left to the rabbit.

The rabbit shares them between her three babies.

They have 3 balls each.

How many balls did I start with?

Take your answer and turn to that page ▶▶

If stuck ▶▶ 66

78

Make a list of all the square numbers, and a list of all the cubes. Keep going until you find a number which appears in both lists.

Squares	Cubes
$2 \times 2 = 4$	$2 \times 2 \times 2 = 8$
$3 \times 3 =$	$3 \times 3 \times 3 =$

Take your answer and turn to that page

If stuck ▶▶ 51

The Magic Mathematician greets you at the Gate of Wisdom.

'Look at your map' he mouths. 'Does it tell you which way to turn so that you can enter through the Gate of Wisdom?'

Yes ▶▶ 76
No PAY 10 POINTS ▶▶ 57

80

Score

480 points | Advance immediately, young novice, to the Expert Mathland. The MM sends you his favourite hat. He hopes it is not too small.
EXCELLENT

400 points | Profound congratulations on a competent journey through the maze. The MM gives you his calculating cap.   **PROFICIENT**

300 points | You met with both success and hardship on your journey, but you came through in the end. The MM awards you with his gold-tipped pencil.   **CAPABLE**

200 points | You have made somewhat erratic progress through the maze, but maybe you will do better next time. The MM gives you his longlife calculator batteries.   **DISMAL**

100 points | The MM is disappointed with your progress. He gives you his correction pen and hopes that you will use it more often in the future.
PATHETIC

Negative | The MM is dumbfounded! Can't you do anything right? He awards you with his wastepaper basket and hopes that you will be comfortable in it!   **DISASTROUS**